Ulterior Motives at The

WHO'S WHO?

Ulterior Motives
The Lost Albums
Lyrics Picture Book

BY CHRISTOPHER & PHILIP BOOTH

DISCLAIMER:
All songs written by Christopher & Philip Booth except Just My Imagination,
Singing In The Rain and To Sir With Love. The Booth Brothers lyrics are
taken from the original writings of the
songwriters and may be slightly different in the recorded material.

Book is attended for mature audiences

Foreword

by Christopher Saint Booth

Being identical twins, Philip and I shared almost everything when we were young, clothes, toys, food and bedrooms. We even had joint custody to Pink Floyd's "The Wall" being that it was a double album. Philip was gifted side one and two and I held the rights to sides three and the flip side. I don't think Philip and I ever got over the fact we shared a bloody album. Definitely a devastating experience for a competitive duo.

The city of Angels, a land of traffic jams and broken

dreams. Welcome to Hollywood, California! Philip and I dared move here to be rock stars. Musicians since the age of 13, we were destined to be noticed whether it was from our outlandish fashion style or the obsession we had for David Bowie, which grew to the point that our hair became spiky orange and eyebrows disappeared by the blades of a razor. We just wanted to be different, you see we just couldn't fit in. Mum would say all the time "Why can't you just be normal?"

Our constant passion led me to become the lead singer and Philip the lead guitar player of London recording artists, gold records, Juno Award Winners,

Sweeney Todd. I had just replaced Bryan Adams as the lead singer. We had a lifestyle that would be hard to end. Along with our older brother Johnny B on drums, we set out on sold out shows and one of the longest tours across Canada.

After the breakup of Sweeney Todd, Philip and I began playing at the local clubs in Los Angeles as the band AlleyBrat. We played many of the legendary venues which included the Starwood, Rainbow, Roxy, Troubadour and the Whiskey. The Hollywood clubs were all about pay to play. I remembering them charging us for tap water in our dressing rooms. We could hardly afford hair spray never mind something to drink.

Times were hard for musicians back then and even harder now, so making a living meant doing anything to survive. Even with the rock band, Mötley Crüe as our opening act (who was not famous at that time), it was hard to make ends meet. That said, we ended up laboring on Hollywood movies for $50.00 dollars a day in the art department. If they needed a ditch dug or a huge billboard moved, we were the ones who did it. Long hours but hey we were still musicians supporting our art. Right? So, we did what we had to do.

Chris remembers working with Charlton Heston and Jack Palance on the sci-fi film "Solar Crisis." In fact if you watch it, I'm the post-apocalyptic trumpet player at the bar. Originally commissioned to design all the futuristic instruments, due to my scruffy look they asked me to appear in the movie. I'm not sure if that was a compliment or not but it lead to my first acting role in a major motion picture.

During the filming of the drama driven movie, "Fear City" starring Tom Berenger and Melanie Griffith, we found the film's budget highlighting the overall costs and job descriptions on the soundstage floor at Raleigh Studios. Like a sign from above or at least the

Hollywood sign, I realized what we needed to do. It was time to get into film production and make our own horror movies. Phil and I had already became well versed in creating music videos and music for Playboy films. They paid better than the indie films and though the scenery was better, the work was dirtier if you know what I mean. We made music that people fast forwarded through when watching such adult entertainment.

**Appearing as a band in some of these films ,
we were called "Affair'.**

Back then Playboy had bigger budgets, better production design and was more story driven than today. They were called Erotic Thrillers. We picked up over 11 Awards worldwide including Best Music. Whether we were working on feature films or adult films, there was not much difference as far as we were concerned. We gave it our all, putting passion in everything and treated every job professionally. For us we were creating art, whether it was music, costuming or production design. During our time with Playboy, we met a lot of nice people, as well as many lost human beings whose spirit and dreams had been broken. We were happy to help make these productions shine. It warmed our heart s to see them transform, be more than they thought they could be. But eventually the productions got cheaper and the content got nastier.

The truth is, it was too difficult on the ego and psyche. we would arrive home after a long day of working, feeling very emotionally exhausted and depressed. We told ourselves we were doing a real film but in reality we were not. Chris states "Being a vegetarian at the time. I had quit drinking and didn't do drugs so I could see things crystal clear. I felt like the actors wore their troubles on the outside as I could see exactly who and what they were. My soul was becoming tarnished, it was time to move on. "

We recorded most of our demos for Who's Who? in Los Angeles, California in a small home studio and a one bedroom apartment belong ing to our dear friend Ricky. May he Rest In Peace. We use an Ensonig Mirage, Korg PolySix, Oberhiem OBX, Farlight and Linn and Simmons Drums and a midi guitar etc.

Chris remembers, "My dear friend Geordie Hormel was the head of the CMI Fairlight division in North America as well as owning the Village Recorder, a recording studio in West Los Angeles. There I met many famous musical artists, such as Robbie Robertson, Peter Gabriel and more. I also helped do some of the keyboard tech work for Keith Emerson, Herbie Hancock as well as do custom sampling on the Fairlight and Emu series."

During one of our recording sessions we had the pleasure to meet, the one an only Michael Jackson. We visited his home in Encino, California, where he took us on a grand tour of his mansion and his pet Lamas. We went on to record a few songs after along with producers George Tobin (Tiffany. Smoky Robinson) and Gary Goetzman (Silence Of The Lambs, Talking heads, UB40). There we scored a record contract with Capitol Records which unfortunately did not pan out due to internal problems with the label. After that we jetted of to London, England where we performed at the Hippodrome, Londons biggest night club and worked with Jett records over there. We wrote our song 'Chemistry' which appeared in the Disney movie, Double Agent.

Michael Jackson & the Booth Brothers

In the 90s we shot a music video. It was called "Like Father, Like Son." The song was about our Dad. The music video was created from the idea of the ultimate father and son, God and his son Jesus. Whether you believe or not, it's a beautiful story of sacrifice and faith. Our team set out to film in Joshua Tree, California where the scenery was similar to that of a biblical location. We filmed for 7 days and 7 nights. In our music video we covered Palm Sunday, the trial, the Stations of the Cross and the crucifixion. Out of all the shots we filmed, the crucifixion was the most powerful of them all. The weather remained good except for the last of day of filming which was the graphic crucifixion scene.Chris remembers the clouds turning black, the rain poured down and lightening flashed. We could hear the rumble of thunder throughout our recordings. It was time to act out the final scene to one of the most important stories of all time. The crew lifted me up onto the 12 foot wooden cross and strapped me in. Made by our prop and set department, it was an exact replica of what would have been used to crucify Jesus back in the day. I must admit I was extremely nervous. It was beyond frightening to act out this religious event. I meant no disrespect in the portrayal, yet I felt I needed to be careful about stepping on sacred ground.

As we started to film, the dark clouds opened up above where I was mounted to the cross. Suddenly a beam of sunlight shone down illuminating me being crucified. My heart dropped with an overwhelming feeling of dread. I remember closing my eyes, even if it was just for a millisecond, I felt the humility, pain, sadness yet faith Jesus must have felt at that time of his sacrifice. It was an incredible life changing moment for me. As I came down from that splintered cross, things now seemed different. Everything was brighter, fresher and more vibrant. I felt a stronger connection to the Earth, its animals, people and the air that we breathe. People of faith would ask me, "How could I receive such a gift that others who have worshiped their whole life had not been given that one moment of true enlightenment?" I'm not sure what happened that day but that Nirvana changed my life. It made me love and care more about everything and everyone. The grass seemed more vibrant in shades of green I had never seen, the cows in the pasture gave off a human-like aura, I could see the air swirl and dance through the sky and smell the crisp, pure aroma as the wind blew past my face. If not for anything else that experience helped me cross my dear Mum as she would pass of cancer that same year. I had seen the trees waving at me, vibrantly protecting themselves from earthly sickness. I had learned that the sap of a Yew Tree held a compound to a possible cure for cancer. I had suggested that my Mum try this experimental drug, as time was running out. This serum of chance bought her a few extra months, which was more than anyone could ask from this horrific fight. Only then could she see the waving of the trees as I had, experiencing this new connection with God together as one. My mother saw the light in me, the Nuns and hospice workers recognized my epiphany. Hand in hand, tear to tear we faced her transition to Heaven. She closed her eyes and the battle was over, finally she found peace. I will always remember when I portrayed Jesus, the day I turned 33 years old.

From music video Like Father Like Son

In memory of Audrey Jackson Booth and Leslie Booth.

Waking up and finding you have one of the most

sought after viral songs on the internet, Ulterior Motives, was a shock for us both. Rolling Stone among

many other music news outlets covered this journey of us and the incredible Lost Media Society who had been searching for our song for over 3 years. With over 56,000 members and millions of people on the search, the rest is history. We set out to bring back all our lost songs form the 80s and early 90s. Going through boxes and boxes of masters, reel to reels, cassettes, CDs and DATs, It was our mission to give to our fans as many songs we could find that had been lost for over 40 years. We appreciate our supporters ever so and will never forget how you all have made us feel, successful and happy. Thank you from the bottom of our hearts.

We have put together this cool book of lyrics and pictures featuring 3 albums of lost music form the 80s and 90s, Volume 1 through 3 containing over 38 songs. We hope you enjoy this as much as we did making them.

Much love Christopher & Philip Booth …..

Christopher and Philip Booth @ Gasparilla Film Festival, Florida

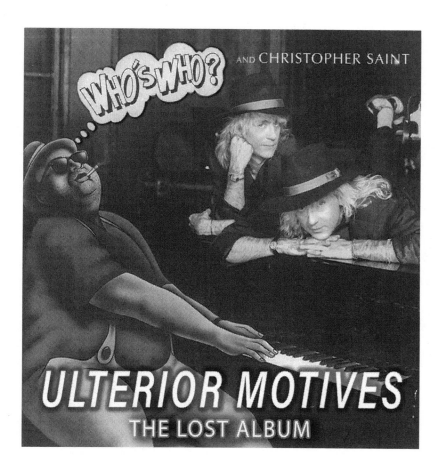

Volume One

Chemistry

I don't mind, If you take your time
I'll handle you slowly
I'll let you get to know me

Our bodies ignite, when we danced tonight
You couldn't get closer if you wanted to

Love is an emotion, It's a powerful potion
You and me got the right chemistry
To make an explosion

Can't you see, the possibility
Two parts you and one part me

If there's some one else
I'll keep my hands to myself
But If your looking my way
I've just got to say

Love is an emotion
It's a powerful potion
You and me got the right chemistry
To make an explosion

Love is an emotion, It's a powerful potion
You and me got the right chemistry

Two parts you and one part me
Oh girl that's chemistry
A lot of you, a bit of me
Shake it up, now that's chemistry

Love is an emotion, It's a powerful potion
You and me got the right chemistry
To make an explosion

Love is an emotion, It's a powerful potion
You and me got the right chemistry
To make an explosion

Your Guy

Hey girl, I love you until the day I die
And forever and ever
I'll be your guy

My mama told me, I'd get over you
My papa told me, find somebody new
People say I will never understand the reason why
You were my girl and I was your guy

Me and you,
Made dreams come true
I don't wanna say goodbye

I wanna be your guy
I wanna be your guy

Do you ever wonder
Who's kissing me now
Who's kissing you now

Have you fallen under
Another guys spell

Don't take it for granted, baby
It's over for good
When I was your guy
Everything was alright

Me and you, made dreams come true
I don't want to say goodbye, oh baby

I wanna be your guy
I wanna be your guy

I'll never forget you girl
That will be the day I die, oh baby

Hey girl, I love you until the day I die
And forever and ever
I will be your guy

I wanna be your guy

Ulterior Motives

Something in your eyes, makes me realize, how
strange it seems
Something in your smile, could be up on trial of
broken dreams
You're counting all your sheep in disguise caught up
in a world of lies

(CHORUS)
Everyone knows it, you've got,
Ulterior Motives

Tell me the truth
Every move shows it, ah ha

Don't you realize, that you're telling lies
Ah ha ha ha ah

If something's on your mind, spit it out and find the
perfect scam
All your truth and dares, do you really care, just who I
am

You're always biting more than you can chew, when
will you realize the truth

Everyone knows it, you've got
Ulterior Motives

Tell me the truth
Every move shows it, ah ha

I got it from the wise that you're telling lies

Everyone knows it (everyone knows it)
You've got Ulterior Motives, tell me the truth

Every move shows it, (every move shows it)

Ah ha ha ha ah

You're always biting more than you can chew
You always saying more than you knew

You're counting all your sheep in disguise
Caught up in a world of lies

(CHORUS OUT)

Man Needs love

I just read the news today
Man needs love right away
Tall and dark, Eyes of blue,
Is looking for a girl like you

Man needs love
Don't you know a man needs love
In a world that's gone crazy,
Man needs love

When the going gets to cold
We all need someone to hold
Got a be a girl for me
Cause man needs love
So desperately

Man needs love
Don't you know a man needs love
In a world that's all gone crazy,
Man needs love

Man needs love
Don't you know a man needs love
Oh girl, girl, Man needs love

Since you left me, things haven't been the same
I know we can work it out, (Work it out maybe)
I pray each night that we work it out
(Work it out baby)
Girl come back to me cause I love you

I won't go, girl don't you see

Man needs love 1, 2, 3

Man needs love
Don't you know a man needs love
In a world that's all gone crazy,

Man needs love
Don't you know a man needs love
You make this man go crazy
Man needs love

So In Love

Don't let our love fade away
Deep in your heart is where I want to stay

Girl what I feel, Kiss me for real
The way you make me feel inside

I just wanna hug, my baby
I'm so in love, so in love
I just wanna kiss, my baby
I need your love

Girl lets make love, I'll light your fire
Your love gets me high
Ow, couldn't get higher

The time is right, I'll take you tonight
You make me come from deep from inside

I just wanna hug, my baby
I'm so in love, so in love
I just wanna kiss, my baby
I need your love, need your love

Oh baby, I just wanna show you baby
A little love and tenderness

Don't let our love fade away
Deep in your heart is where I want to stay, ow

Girl what I feel, I know it's for real
The way you make me feel inside

I just wanna hug, my baby
I'm so in love, so in love
I just wanna kiss, my baby
I need your love
I just want a hold, everything that turns to gold
So in love
I just want a hug, my baby, I need your love, need
your love

M - y - b - a - b - y, don't you know you make me cry

You Turn Me On

Hey I'm looking you over
Let's take a chance
I just want to walk over
And ask you to dance
Come on girl let's get it on

You turn me on baby
Like no one else can
You make me hot, sugar
I melt in your hands
You turn me on baby
I'm coming inside

I want to kiss you all over
I wanna eat you alive
Do it to me slower
Make me last all night
Feel your body
Come on girl, Let's get it on

You turn me on baby
Like no one else can
You make me hot, sugar
I melt in your hands
You turn me on baby
Keep turning me on

You turn me on baby
Like no one else can
You make me hot, sugar
Make me your man
You turn me on baby

I'm coming inside
You make me wet, darling

You turn me on baby
Like no one else can
You make me hot, sugar
Make me your man
You turn me on baby

You turn me on

Rock Me To Sleep

You got the power, you got the energy
Even in my wildest dreams
So don't wake me up, Rock me to sleep

Ooh, tell me baby, That this is not a dream
Ooh, would you love me baby, You make me wanna
scream

Ooh, you got the power, To move me in my jeans

When I dreaming your mine to keep, baby
So don't wake me up, Rock me to sleep

(CHORUS)
Even in my wildest dreams
I'll fall in love with you
Even in my wildest dreams
I hope these dreams come true

Oh can I pinch your body, To see if your for real
Oh, will you touch me baby
Cause I love the way it feels

When I'm dreaming I'm wetting the sheets
so don't wake me up, Rock me to sleep

Even in my wildest dreams
I'll fall in love with you
Even in my wildest dreams
I hope these dreams come true

Even in my wildest dreams
I'll do anything for you
Anything you wanna
Even in my wildest dreams
I hope these dreams come true

When I'm dreaming, I'm wetting the sheets
So don't wake me up, Rock me to sleep

(Repeat chorus)

Think I'm Gonna Cry

Dear lover tell me the truth
Do you think about me
Like I think about you

Baby, I think I'm gonna cry

Feel my heart break every time your near
Intimate moments baby
I shed the tears

Baby, I think I'm gonna cry

How could love be so blind
I thought you weren't the hurting kind
How could love be so cruel
And leave me crying like a fool

Dear lover, You said were forever
There's sunshine when we're loving baby
Now there just stormy weather

Baby, I think I'm gonna cry

Cry like a baby

How could love be so kind
And take away what was mine
The game of love has no rules
How can I win, when I always lose
I think I'm gonna cry like a baby

Taste The Potion Of Emotion

Pretend your mine, A gold mine, and your all mine to
hide
It's crossed my mind, that loves blind, it would break
my stride

We could build a life from a dream
One way or another, the smells sweet when we hurt
each other

Now we taste the potion of emotion
Now we taste the potion of devotion

What's your sign, is there no sign of sunshine
shinning through
What's your line, am I in line with a white wine, I
drink to you

We should quench the thirst of a stream
If it's one thing it's another, It smells sweet when we
hurt each other

Now we taste the potion of emotion
Now we taste the potion of devotion

Now we taste the potion of emotion
Now we taste the potion of devotion

We could build a life from a dream
One taste of another, there's a world you've never
seen

I don't know how to say
What has to be said
It's now or never
Keeps going through my head

Now we taste the potion of emotion
Now we taste the potion of devotion
Now we taste the potion of emotion
Now we taste the potion of devotion

One Last Look

I know your going somewhere
I can see it in your eyes

That when tomorrow comes
There will be photos ripped and torn
With tears

One last look won't last forever
One last look into your eyes

Can I see you on the weekends
Is it me or your career

My heart is like, A broken camera, with tears

One last look won't last forever
One last look into your eyes

One last look won't last
One last look won't last

One last look won't last forever

They say I'm going nowhere
Since you've left
Since you're gone
My life is like a fatal accident
Without one last look

One last look won't last forever
One last look into your eyes

Nothing Lasts Forever

I tried to hide my feelings, they're sliding through my
hands
It keeps me with a reason, when it's time to
understand
We were forever, Well we just might of been
But the ones who hide from never, are always in
between

Nothing lasts forever,
Not the rain or the shining stars in your eyes Nothing
lasts forever,
So there's your alibi

Now who's heart is healing, and who's minds on the
mend
That goodnight kiss your feeling, You'll have to find a
friend
Cause I'm not taking no more, I had more than I can
take
I'm not betting on the game, there's too much
mistake

Nothing lasts forever,
Not the rain or the shining stars in your eyes Nothing
lasts forever,
So there's your alibi

Nothing lasts forever,
Not the rain or the shining stars in your eyes Nothing
lasts forever, So bye, bye baby

Oh I can't let go, when your in my life, your all I
know
But now you should go, for nothing lasts forever,
Cause some things will never change

I tried to hide my feelings, they're sliding through my
hands
It keeps me with a reason, when it's time to
understand
We were forever, Well we just might of been
But the ones who hide from never, is always in
between

Nothing lasts forever,
Not the rain or the shining stars in your eyes
Nothing lasts forever, bye, bye baby, So there's your
alibi
Nothing lasts forever,
Not the rain or the shining stars in your eyes
Nothing lasts forever, bye, bye baby, So there's your
alibi

Nothing lasts forever,
Nothing, Nothing

Language Of Love

How to say, Something that's been said so many ways
I don't want to be like all the rest

The road is long, Everybody says that we went wrong
Don't listen what they say
I love you more each day
Girl it hurts so much, When you're gone, oh

Finding the right words to say
Is learning the language
Your getting closer everyday
To speaking the language of love

No one can take your place
Every girl wears your face
The language of love

I can't feel, Something deep inside feels so real
Don't know what to do, just got to talk to you
Girl you got to know how I feel

(CHORUS)
Finding the right words to say
Is learning the language of love
Your getting closer everyday
To speaking the language of love

Weather it's wrong or right
I know I need you tonight
The language of love
Whisper three words in my ear
You learn from the heart not the tears

Finding the right words to say
Is learning the language
Your getting closer everyday
I'm speaking the language of love

Tell me the words you hear
whisper them in my ears
The language of love

(Chorus repeat)

Lie School

I'm your man your new exam
Your latest tragedy
The school of truth
Thinks your uncouth
So skip the honesty

When you lied to me
You earned your degree in,

Lie school, Lie school
Honesty broke the golden rule in,
Lie school, Lie school
Where you learned to lie

Basic math gone psycho path
But girl don't count on me
Alimony, equals lonely
9 out of 10 agree

When you lied to me
You earned your degree in,

Lie school, Lie school
Honesty broke the golden rule in,
Lie school, Lie school
Where you learned to lie
Lie school, lie school
Lie school, it's gonna make you lie

I'm your man your new exam
Teachers pet to be

Kiss the guys and make them lie
Give it all in modesty
From ABC to lie.... in,

Lie school, Lie school
Honesty broke the golden rule in,
Lie school, Lie school

It's gonna make you lie

Volume Two

Love Letters

A is anything you do, b is just being next to you,
C is crazy, d is dumb, e is easy, f's for fun

Oh, write me tonight, oh

G is gleaming like a star, h is hot that's what you are
I love you and you love me, j is just okay with me

Oh, write me tonight, oh

So go ahead and, write love letters
It's gonna make you feel a lot better
So go ahead and, write love letters
And seal it with a kiss now baby

K is kissing in the dark, L is loving with all your heart
M, n, o, p, come on baby write to me

Oh, write me tonight, oh

So go ahead and, write love letters
It's gonna make you feel a lot better
So go ahead and, write love letters
And seal it with a kiss now baby

A -adore, B-baby, C-caring, D-darling, E-easy, F-fun,
G-giving, H-hot, I-I love you, J-just for you, K-
kissing,
L-love letters, M-maybe, N-no way, O-oou,
P-passion, Q, R, S, T, U, V, X, Y, Z

LOVE LETTERS

Oh, write me tonight, oh

So go ahead and, write love letters
It's gonna make you feel a lot better
So go ahead and, write love letters
And seal it with a kiss now baby

Animal In Me

Performed by AFFAIR

You love me and I love you tonight
In the morning we'll just kiss and say goodbye
The moon was full, I was feeling like a man
Hoping tonight is enough

Loving you was meant to last
I came on too fast
Must have been the animal in me

I met you and you met me
We were meant to be
Feeling you holding me
Is all I ever need

When you walked in my life
I was looking for a thrill
Now I'm in for the kill

Loving you was meant to last
I came on too fast
Must have been the animal in me
I want you to know, I'll never hurt you so
Help me tame the animal in me

You love me and I love you tonight
In the morning we'll go our separate ways
Goodnight
It's only instinct deep down inside
Don't run away and hide

Loving you was meant to last

I came on too fast
Must have been the animal in me
I want you to know, I'll never hurt you so
Help me tame the animal in me

Loving you was meant to last
I came on too fast
Must have been the animal in me

All For Love

You and I was meant to be
C'mon baby dance with me
I hear you found someone new
He won't treat you, like I do

If you did it all again
Would you see other men
No one else would ever do
All the things I've done for you

All for love, I did it
Theres nothing i can do about it
All for love, I did it

All for love, I did it
Girl I can't live without it
All your love

All is fair in love and war
Girl lets even up the score
I did it all for love

Don't know why I should stay
When all you do is run, run away, baby
I love you girl with all my heart
Even when we're apart
No matter what you put me through
Girl I gave my all to you

All for love, I did it

There's nothing I can do about it
All for love, I did it

All for love, I did it
Girl I can't live without it
All your love

You and I was meant to be
Come on baby, make love to me
I hear you found someone new
He won't treat you, like I do you

If we did it all again
Would there be a happy end
No one else will ever do
All the things I've done for you

All for love, I did it
There's nothing I can do about it
All for love, I did it

All for love, I did it
Girl I can't live without it
All your love

My Sweetheart

Darling let our love keep on shinning

Baby lovers road is long and winding

I told you I'd hold you, Till death do us part

How can I, How can I, How can I, go wrong

My Sweetheart, My Sweetheart

Darling, stop my heart from breaking

With hugging and kissing and lots of love making

I promise to cherish you with all of my heart

How can I, How can I, How can I, go wrong

My Sweetheart, My Sweetheart

Darling let our love keep on shining

Baby lovers road, is so long and winding

I never loved anyone the way I do you

How can I, How can I, How can I, go wrong

My Sweetheart, My Sweetheart
My Sweetheart
Darling

She Loves Me, She Loves Me Not

If you play with fire, old flames burn much brighter
than new ones do

One's desire helps me tame the liar inside of you

Ouu she loves me, she loves me not

Ouu she loves me, she loves me not

You said you need me, you change your mind and
leave me

Now that takes time

Its time to release me, for in my sleep you're near me,
now that's a sign

If you ever knew how much I wanted you,

You don't know what you have until it's gone

I won't be the one that comes to you, oh

Ouu she loves me, she loves me not

Ouu she loves me, she loves me not

Aye-yeah

Ouu she loves me, she loves me not

Aye-yeah

Let me be the one you're running too, oh

Let me be the one

Ouu she loves me, she loves me not

Ouu she loves me, she loves me not

Ouu she loves me, she loves me not

Ouu she loves me, she loves me not

In Other Words

You never said that you loved me It was on the tip of,
my tongue
All that we touched, I can't believe, I didn't mean
that much
Why don't you just put your arms around me

In other words, I could be happy
Three words, make our dreams come true
In other words, We could be happy

I carry around an empty feeling
You carry around what love has made

Love is a word, If it's blind than it should be heard
A kiss is a kiss, that made a child that we both miss
Why don't you just put your life in my shoes

In other words, I could be happy
Three words, make dreams come true

In other words, We could be happy
If these three words are, I LOVE YOU

Why don't you just put your arms around me and
hold me
When you said we were over, I felt my heart drop to
my knees

The last time I felt this
Was the first time that we kissed

In time the hurt will let me forget you

In other words, I could be happy
Three words, make our dreams come true

In other words, We could be happy
If these words are I love you

In other words, You could be happy
Three words make our dreams come true

In other words, We all could be happy, so happy,

If these three words are, I LOVE YOU

3 Blind Mice

I wish I knew, which way to turn
When one loves two, someone gets burned by love

Well I choose you, but my heart won't see There's a
girl back at home missing me

When you love more than one
You know it's wrong

We're just like 3 blind mice
Running round in circles, that don't think twice
We're like 3 Blind Mice

There's a time in my life, that I will find
If she comes to mind, let the blind lead the blind,
Fall in love

Show me a sign, so I may choose
But love is blind and I'll miss the one I lose

What you feel deep inside
Helps me decide
We're just like 3 blind mice
Running round in circles, that don't think twice
We're like 3 blind mice

3 Blind Mice, 3 Blind Mice
3 Blind Mice, 3 Blind Mice

At the end when you're gone
No ones lost, No ones won
Let me be the one

We're just like 3 Blind Mice
Running round in circles, that don't think twice
We're like 3 Blind Mice

We're just like 3 blind mice
Running round in circles, that don't think twice
We're like 3 Blind Mice

Shiver

Go with that gut feeling
But know the heart you're stealing
The icy chill of love tingles down my spine

To have someone to rely on
A shoulder to cry on
A lover to spy on

Don't it make you Shiver, Shiver
Don't it make you Shiver, Shiver

You want someone to save you
Well the odds are in your favor
The touch of another, no longer cross my mind

To have someone, I can talk to
A doorway, I could walk through
A white house and a picket fence
Like a fairy tale with a happy end

When you care about somebody
Really care about somebody

Don't it make you Shiver, Shiver
Don't it make you cry
Don't it make you Shiver, Shiver
Don't it make you wonder why

Don't it make you Shiver, Shiver
Don't it make you die
Don't it make you Shiver, Shiver
Don't it make you wonder why

Shiver

Don't it make you Shiver, Shiver
Don't it make you cry
Don't it make you Shiver, Shiver
Don't it make you wonder why

Don't it make you Shiver, Shiver
Don't it make you cry

We Can Live On Love

Bills are high and moneys low
All I know is I got you girl

There's no jobs around, but don't get down
Cause we can live on love

We can live on love, Ooh, come on girl
We can live on love, Ooh

No matter how things may be
I got you and you got me
Cause we can live on love

Times are tough, can't make enough
I've worked so hard to keep you baby
I'd give you everything, that money can't buy
Cause we can live on love

We can live on love, Ooh, come on girl
We can live on love, Ooh
With that precious love you bring
We can face anything, we can live on love

I didn't know it, I didn't know it
That the best things in life are free
Thats you and me, baby

Ah - yeah
Anything you could ever want, I can give it
We can live on love , Ooh, come on girl
We can live on love, Ooh
No matter how things may be

I got you and you got me
We can live on love

We can't live on love, Ooh, come on girl
We can live on love , Ooh

Our love might not pay the rent
But our love is heaven cent
We can live on love

Who's The Other Guy?

Ooh ooh ooh ooh ooh ooh ooh ooh ooh ooh

Where'd I go wrong
We had a good thing going girl
But now you gone
I can't understand, I can see it in your eyes
You found another man

Love me love me not
Oh why won't you tell me
What's he got that I don't got

Who's the other guy, I wonder
Who's the other guy you love
Who's the other guy, baby
Who's the other guy

What more can I say
I cannot do anything girl to make you stay
But one day you'll see
Never be anyone who'll love you more than me

Tell you from my heart
I'll always remember
Got to know before we part

Who's the other guy, I wonder
Who's the other guy, you love
Who's the other guy, baby
Who's the other guy
Who's the other guy
Who's the other guy I wonder

Oooh noooo nooo oooh ooh ooh ooh

So where'd I go wrong
I gave you everything I have
And now you gone

Ooh ooh ooh ooh ooh ooh ooh ooh ooh ooh

Who's the other guy? I wonder

Who's the other guy, baby
Who's the other guy, I wonder
Who's the other guy, baby
Ooh ooh ooh ooh
Who's the other guy, baby

Just One Touch

I didn't know when you walked into my life
You'd cut deep like a blade of a knife
You're running me hot, you're making me steam
I know I've met you before in a dream

Just one touch, that's all it took to need you so much
Just one touch, that's all it took, that's all it took

Stormy weather on the chart, I'd try and stop before
I start
I'm only saying what's in my heart

When you're away, I'm lost but I found
That you built a fire that can't be put out
I've never felt this way before
I'm like a cat, Eye need to explore

Just one touch, that's all it took to need you so much
Just one touch, that's all it took, a touch to much

Just one touch, I never thought I'd miss you so much
Just one touch, that's all it took, that's all it took

Stormy weather on the chart, I'd try and stop before
I start
I'm only saying what's in my heart
So you just push, and I will shove, I'll put on a silver
glove
I'll put a g in front of love

I didn't know when you walked into my life, you'd cut
deep like a blade of a knife

When you live with a dream, You know you'll awake
I guess that's the chance, I've gotta take

Just one touch, that's all it took to need you so much
Just one touch, that's all it took, a touch to much
And you can push and I will shove, I'll put a g in front
of love

Just one touch, I never thought I'd miss you so much
Just one touch, that's all it took, that's all it took,

Stormy weather on the chart, I'd try and stop before
I start
I'm only saying what's in my heart

Till the end of time

Performed by AFFAIR

Tick Tock
You be my job
I'll be your pay
We'll work all night, all day

You be my act
I'll be your stage
We can act out our play

I'll be your friend
I'll be your man
I'll be yours, till the end of time

Till the end of
Till the end of
Till the end of

Till the end of Time

Tick Tock
You be my crime
And I'll get involved
We can be the case, that's unsolved

You be the stone
I'll be the glass
Together we'll break the past

I'll be your man
I'll be your friend
I'll be I'll be yours, till the end of time

Till the end of
Till the end of
Till the end of

Till the end of Time

Just My Imagination

(Norman Whitfield and Barrett Strong)

Yeah, Um Baby
Each day through my window, I watch her as she
passes by
I say to myself, "You're such a lucky guy"
To have a girl like her is truly a dream come true
Out of all the guys in the world, she chose you

But it was just my imagination
Running' away with me
It was just my imagination, Oh baby
Running' away with me

JustMy Imagination, Just, Just My Imagination

Ooh (Soon)
Soon we'll be married and raise a family (Oh yeah)
A cozy little home out in the country
With two children, maybe three
I can visualize it all
This couldn't be a dream, for it seems much too real

But it was just my imagination, once again
Running' away with me
It was just my imagination, Oh baby
Just Just, Just Just, Just My Imagination

Each day at my window, I die as she passes by
I say to myself, "You're such a lucky guy"

But don't you know, It's Just my imagination

Once again
Running' away with me, Ah

It's just my imagination, oh yeah
Just my imagination, Just Just, Ah baby
Running' away with me

Just my imagination, Just Just my imagination
Just my imagination, Just Just my imagination

Modern Heroes
Volume Three

To Sir With Love

Written by **Mark London** and Don Black
Performed by ALLEYBRAT

Those schoolgirl days
Of telling tales and biting nails are gone

But in my mind
I know they will still live on and on

But how do you thank someone
Who has taken you from crayons to perfume?
It isn't easy, but I'll try

If you wanted the sky
I would write across the sky in letters
That would soar a thousand feet high
"To sir, with love"

The time has come
For closing books and long last looks must end
And as I leave
I know that I am leaving my best friend

A friend who taught me right from wrong
And weak from strong
That's a lot to learn
What, what can I give you in return?

If you wanted the moon
I would try to make a start
But I would rather you let me give my heart
"To sir, with love"

May Day In Heaven

I know the bottom line when the arrows pointing up
Send no valentines, I can read an empty cup
She said what's a matter with you
I said what's a matter with me
Bon Voyage, relationship

May day in heaven, Our ship is on the rocks
If she gives you the cold shoulder, head back to the
docks

May day in heaven, our ship is in distress,
We've got a love that's made in heaven send out a sos

I know wrong from my right
But my left keep an eye on
Loves like bird in the sky
Salt n pepper, It's an egg on

She said what's a matter with you
I said what's a matter with me
Bon voyage, relationship

May day in heaven, Our ship is on the rocks
If she gives you the cold shoulder, head back to the
docks

May day in heaven, our ship is in distress,
We've got a love that's made in heaven
Send out a SOS...

Apologies, The best policy , Not honesty

I know what's in store, when you toss me a line
I'll go ship to shore, I'm just the guy who had his time

She said what's a matter with you
I said what's a matter with me
Bon voyage, relationship

May day in heaven, Our ship is on the rocks
If she gives you the cold shoulder, head back to the
docks

May day in heaven, our ship is in distress,
We've got a love that's made in heaven

For All We know

Don't try now

To understand the perfect crime
To know what's yours, is mine

Don't try now

For all we know
Your ring of fire is burning cold

For all we care
When he stole your heart, he stole the coal

He stole the coal
He stole the coal

It feeds the fire

It feeds the soul

For all we know

For all we know

Don't cry now

Love is such a funny game
Roll the ice into the flame

Don't cry now for him
He's like an ocean swim

Singing In The Rain

(written by Nacio Herb Brown (music) and Arthur Freed)

Performed by ALLEYBRAT

I'm singing in the rain, just singing in the rain

What a glorious feeling, I'm happy again

I'm laughing at clouds so dark up above

The sun's in my heart and I'm ready for love

Let the stormy clouds chase everyone from the place

Come on with the rain, I've a smile on my face

I walk down the lane with a happy refrain

Just singing, singing in the rain

Dancing in the rain

I'm happy again

I'm singing and dancing in the rain

I'm dancing and singing in the rain

We Are The Future

Performed by ALLEYBRAT

You know I reach for a drink
whenI get out of bed
Sometimes all I can do is
a gun to my head

Slip on my red vinyl suit and my black bowler cap
Then I'm out on the street ready to attack

We are the English mod an army with a style
To fight society and do it with a smile
A wink of painted eye as you slide from hand to hand
when we rape your respect do you know who I am

We are the future, We are the future
We are the English mod you are the one that's odd
We are the shapes of things to come

I know it's hard for you to understand anything I do

We are the future, We are the future
We are the English mod, you are the one that's odd
We are the shape of things to come

Future, Future, will I see
We are the shapes of things to be,

We are, We are, We are, We are
You punk

More To Come......

The Interviews

Their Song Spawned an Internet Mystery. Now They're Ready to
Tell Their Story. BY MILES KLEE

After moving to L.A. in the 1980s, Christopher and Philip Booth broke into the movie business by scoring adult films — and one of their tracks went viral decades later.

It took <u>years of searching</u> and too many false leads to count, but the musicians behind the mysterious 1980s pop tune commonly referred to as "Everyone Knows That" or "EKT" — the real title is "Ulterior Motives" <u>have been identified</u>: Christopher Saint Booth sang the vocals on the beguiling track, while his identical twin brother Philip Adrian Booth played the guitar. It was originally part of the soundtrack on the 1986 adult film *Angels of Passion*, one of several porn flicks the pair scored in their youth before embarking on long and fruitful moviemaking careers of their own.

Ever since an anonymous person with the handle "carl92" uploaded a low-quality, 17-second sample of it to WatZatSong in 2021, "Ulterior Motives" has fascinated the forensic audio detectives of the "lost-wave" community, hobbyists who track down the source of compelling music snippets that have survived outside their original context and without credits. Thanks to its infectious hook and a sound that tapped into a deep well of nostalgia, it became one of the most highly sought sonic artifacts in this online world, with tens of thousands collaborating on a <u>subreddit</u> to figure out who had made it and, just as importantly, how to track down a complete recording.

The Booth brothers had long forgotten the track and, until a few days ago, remained completely unaware that a fragment of it lived on as a viral hit. Once a couple of redditors <u>cracked the case</u> and named them as the musicians behind it, they were deluged with phone messages and comments on <u>social media</u> they couldn't quite understand at first. After this outreach by fans and friends, the siblings began to grasp the impact of their lost work and appreciate the lengths people had gone to recover it. Here, they speak to *Rolling Stone* about how "Ulterior Motives" came into existence, the pleasure of having it salvaged from the sands of time, and plans to release a polished version of the single as a way of saying thanks — along with more of the glitzy pop music they wrote back then.

So, how are you?

Christopher: I'm fabulous! Just swamped and blown away by this situation, never even knew about it till two days ago.

Philip: We were just flabbergasted. I mean, we had no idea this was going back to 2021, to be honest.

How did you find out?

Christopher: We used to work for SyFy channel for like 10 years, doing paranormal documentaries, and we did horror movies for Sony and stuff. We did [a documentary called *The Exorcist File*, about the case that inspired the novel *The Exorcist*]. And I was posting promo for that, then people started writing "release EKT" or "Ulterior Motives," and I'm going, "What's that?" I didn't remember the song at all, that's 40 years ago. And then it got crazy. Someone sent me a link to <u>your article</u> [about lost-wave sleuths looking for the complete song]. And then I went, "Oh, yeah." Then I heard the song and I went "Oh yeah, that's us." That's how we found out.

Philip: I have to tell you, on a human level, it really brought deep emotion and tears to our eyes to see so many kids singing the song, saying how great the song was. There's just no better feeling as a musician to see such gratification for something. They discovered our names, our phones started blowing up, social media started blowing up. You know, we're not big TikTok followers — my daughter wrote me and said, "Dad, I'm so proud of you. You're all over TikTok. And we're all singing the song." I thought, "Oh, my God, what's happening?"

That's an amazing moment. And this song was so early in your careers, you were just getting started, right?

Christopher: We were in a very successful rock & roll band called Sweeney Todd, which was out of Canada, they did a big hit song called "Roxy Roller." Bryan Adams replaced [original lead vocalist] Nick Gilder, and then Bryan Adams actually was fired. I was hired as a singer and Phil played guitar. [Another Booth brother, John, played drums.] We made our way to America, and started playing [L.A. venues] the Rainbow [Bar], the Whiskey [a Go Go]. Mötley Crüe backed us up, because we were a very heavy rock band.

Philip: This was the very early Eighties.

Christopher: So "Ulterior Motives" was recorded around 1986, it was recorded as a pop song, and then to make money — we were just doing anything to make money, because we were musicians. Even worse today, trying to make any money. We took jobs working on movies like as production assistants, in the art department, we did some really big films. And then there was a friend of ours that was doing adult movies and they needed somebody to do craft services and move stuff around.

Philip: We were in our early twenties.

Christopher: And we knew the producers, who were very nice, and they needed music. They gave us quite a bit of money just to give them some music to use behind the scenes. And of course we needed the money. So that's how that happened. Despite some people saying was never written for an adult film. It was actually written as a pop song, and we just used it in there.

I think there were a lot of people who didn't think it could be from an adult film because nobody making adult films today really bothers with that stuff anymore.

Philip: Honestly, back then, the industry was completely different. They were making actual films and stories and shooting on film.

Christopher: Their budgets were like 10 or 15 grand back then.

Philip: Nowadays, it's just, you know, a camcorder or phone or whatever, but back then it was a huge industry. And we learned, actually, from licensing music for them to use, working on the sets. We learned how to shoot film, and we got the bug, and that's how we ended up wanting to make movies, not adult movies, but *movies*. By seeing how exciting that was, with film cameras and lights. We were produced by Smokey Robinson's producer, Gary Goetzman, back in the Eighties, who did *Stop Making Sense* with David Byrne. He heard the songs that were coming out, and he loved it. He took us in to get a record deal, and we released a couple of songs. But all these other songs [including "Ulterior Motives"] were lost songs. We had a whole album of this Eighties stuff. You know, that music back then just had such fun about it. It had such melody and innocence, so to see people nowadays singing it and what they're saying about it, we're just blown away.

You recorded this 40 years ago — what was it like to listen to it again?

Philip: The first thing was said was, "What are we going to do? They want a new version, a clean version, a remastered version ... "

Christopher: It actually put tears in our eyes. It was so beautiful. Music is a very touching thing. I've always been a musician, I still do music for films, and music is my life. I own a very big studio, Pro Tools, the whole thing. I do nothing but Atmos surround sound for films, but I've always written pop songs. Philip and I liked George Michael and Culture Club back then. And then Nine Inch Nails and Peter Gabriel influenced us. To go back [to the song] felt like we were 20 again.

Philip: I can't tell you how exciting it was to see so many young people singing that song, going out their way to record those songs. There is no greater high for a musician than to see that it stands the test of time. So what we decided is we've got to go in the studio and start figuring out what we're going to do now.

It would be amazing if you could perform it live at one of those old clubs on the Sunset Strip.

Philip: Is the Viper Room dead now? Is it closed?

No, it's still around! I saw a heavy metal show there not long ago. They're still rocking.

Philip: We remember going to see the Babys at the Roxy [Theatre]. When we were playing, we played the Troubadour.

Christopher: This was a little after the writing of that song, because we were into synth-wave back then. We were moving into heavy rock at that point, because we've gone through every genre of music — except for country, of course. Music is probably the best fountain of youth ever.

Do you remember what inspired the lyrics for "Ulterior Motives"?

Christopher: Yeah, it was a girl that cheated. She was saying one thing and you found out that she did another thing.

Philip: It went viral as "EKT," for "everyone knows that." We posted the lyrics and the fans said, "Oh my god, it's 'everyone knows *it*,' not 'everyone knows *that*.'"

Christopher: We've got to go through 40 years of tapes to see if we can find it, and if we can't find it, we're gonna go ahead and rerecord it. I might have to squeeze my balls to sing that high now. We have been able to find the rhythm track, and we're looking for the vocal track right now. If not, we're very prepared to go in and redo it and do it as close as possible to the original but with a modern recording sound, so the quality is right up to par with today's sound. I'm gonna take it in there and give everybody what they want. Whether it bombs or not, I don't know, but I don't think we can *not* do it.

Philip: It's like being Peter Gabriel or Guns N' Roses, anybody who writes new material, but they all want to hear that old song from 40 years ago! I think you have to please your fans. You can't be so self-absorbed. I have to say, I didn't realize how catchy this song is. And now it's like, I can't stop singing it. The beauty of it is we're starting to go through the music and have discovered a whole album's worth of music written back then that sounds like that. And everybody's saying, "You need to put that album out." It's changed our life.

Christopher: It's extra energy to get you out of bed, it really is.

Philip: We just don't want to pass up this thing. It's bigger than us now.

Have you checked out other stuff in the lost-wave scene?

Christopher: I haven't had chance to, because it's still been very overwhelming. I did read the articles and Reddit, tried to follow a lot of TikTok stories and YouTube videos to understand what the whole community's about.

Philip: I heard that carl92 went into hiding because he couldn't admit he heard [the song] in an adult film. [*Editor's note: It's not clear how the anonymous poster, who later disappeared from WatZatSong, obtained the recording he shared in 2021, claiming he had found it on a "DVD backup" from when he was learning to capture audio.*] Well, I think we owe a really big thank you to carl92. We had to call our brother who was in Sweeney Todd with us, Johnny B., we had to tell him, "You remember that song?" He says "Yeah." I tell him I just saw an article in *Rolling Stone* and had to send it to him. He's a diehard musician from the day, and we always had huge respect for *Rolling Stone*. We said to Johnny B., the three of us gotta get these tracks back. This kind of stuff just doesn't happen. There's got to be a bigger picture behind why this happened. And so we're thrilled, and we want to thank everybody, and we want to share the excitement.

What can you tell the fans about that other unreleased material?

Christopher: We have found a lot of tracks that we worked on with a producer that used to do Tiffany and New Edition. That's what they were trying to make us sound like back then, and they produced it really well. We even did covers, like "Just My Imagination," which is actually a beautiful cover of the Temptations song. They're in studio quality and I can remaster them. As far as "Ulterior Motives," we have the rhythm track and we're going to throw the guitar track back on there, it's an Eighties synthesizer guitar.
Philip: Everybody was asking, "How'd you get that

guitar sound?" Back then there used to be something called a MIDI guitar. And what you do with a MIDI guitar is you have two feeds: One puts the distortion of guitar sound out of the jack, and the other triggers a keyboard. So when you're playing, it's playing keyboard sounds at the same time.

Christopher: I'm gonna redo the vocals and I can pretty much do it, even though I sounded like a 13-year-old girl back then. But that's the sound they were going for, New Edition.

Philip: We had some people on TikTok and YouTube dissecting it, filtering it.

Christopher: Yeah, apparently I'm a Japanese girl.

Philip: [Imitating a lost-wave sleuth] "At first I thought it was a male, but after my detective work I can hear by the accent that it's a Japanese girl." We're just laughing like, "Oh, god."

Christopher: So what we're gonna do is release the song, and if people like it and they want to hear more, we're prepared to release a whole album of tracks that sound a lot like that — Culture Club, Depeche Mode, George Michael, ABC, everyone in the Eighties we were influenced by. We actually went to England to do a record deal, we were signed to Capitol Records for that kind of stuff. For whatever reason, there was something that just didn't work out with the deal. So we ended up making movies instead. Still doing music, but movies were making more money at the time.

Do you still have all that old tech you used?

Philip: I still have the MIDI guitar; I brushed the dust off it yesterday. We're gonna make a couple of videos.

Christopher: You put things out in the universe — recently I just got into this thought of getting all these old Seventies synthesizers back. I don't know why. I've just been obsessed with bringing them back, you know, the Moog. I used to work for Keith Emerson as a as a keyboard tech. I just started bringing all these keyboards into my studio, and I think it channeled the universe.

Philip: We still have a lot of that oldest gear, the old classic Linn Drum machine. The detectors were saying, "We found that it was a Linn Drum machine." And it's so cool, how deep they get into this stuff. But I think they want that Eighties sound anyway. If we have to re-create anything, we'll use the original equipment.

What will your band name be when you release this material?

Philip: I don't know, you might need to help us on that. We were trying to figure out what we were going by back then. And because we're identical twin brothers. We had a band called Who's Who? Everybody used to come up to us and say, "Who's who?" You should see some of the promo stuff we had. The pictures are amazing, with the hair and everything.

Christopher: Maybe a can of hairspray would be a good cover.

I mean, even "Ulterior Motives" would be a great name. You've got options.

Christopher: Maybe the fans can help us figure that out. What we didn't want to do was let anybody down. I know a lot of people spent a lot of time and [showed a lot of] support for many to be involved in all this. So we're gonna go ahead and release it, and hopefully, they'll dig it. But we love it and we appreciate them.

It's really special, and it speaks to the power of art — that people found this snippet and said, "It's not right that I can't hear the rest of this song. This song deserves to be known, and the people who made it deserve to be known."

Philip: And it was only a 17-second snippet.

Christopher: We're pretty excited about it. We do movies and TV shows; we do very well doing that. And I do soundtracks for movies and my own albums as well, I have one out now called *SkyPolar*, which is reminiscent of old synthesizers, like Emerson, Lake & Palmer, and Pink Floyd, mixing Hans Zimmer with Nine Inch Nails-type stuff. So we didn't really need to [revisit "Ulterior Motives"], but we feel like we need to do it as a thank you to everyone who took their time over the years of looking for it. We need to do that for them.

RAGS (Late 70s)

"Ulterior Motives" Singers Christopher Saint Booth and Philip Adrian Booth on Viral Fame and Giving Fans What They Want. By Russ Burlingame

COMICBOOK

A "lost song" was discovered last month, and now the veteran musicians and filmmakers behind it are preparing its first-ever official release.

Last month, an enduring internet mystery was solved when fans figured out the "lost-wave" song known colloquially as "Everyone Knows That" was in fact a 1980s song called "Ulterior Motives" by British-Canadian filmmakers Christopher Saint Booth and Philip Adrian Booth. The duo wrote the song in 1986, and sold it to an adult film that same year. It was never commercially released outside of the context of the movie, and was a footnote in their career, which involved years in pop music followed by years making film and TV projects, largely in the horror genre. Then, on April 28, 2024, they discovered that a group of passionate fans had been obsessed with the song for a couple of years.

A 17-second clip from the song was posted to song identification website WatZatSong in 2021 by a user with the handle Carl92. Carl said he found the snippet mixed in with some old DVD backups, and that he had likely recorded it off the TV and used it to teach himself audio editing. Years later, he wanted to listen to the song in full, but had no idea where it came from.

"I saw on one of the [Instagram] posts for – we make motion pictures and TV shows, and do all the music – it was a weird post, and I thought it was maybe, possibly trolling," Christopher Saint Booth told ComicBook. "I didn't really get it – it didn't connect for me. And then somebody had sent me, 'Don't you know? Check out Reddit. Check out *Rolling Stone*.' And then I looked at it and I said, 'Okay.' And then I clicked on that pink boombox and I was like, 'Oh my God, that's our song.' That's how we figured it out. I'm still finding out things today that were posted many, many years ago that is blowing me away."

The pink boombox in question is the NextPlay "Glitz and Glitter" boombox. Released in the mid-2000s, the sparkly, pink-and-white boombox has become closely associated with "Ulterior Motives," with a photo of one having been used as the thumbnail image in one of the most widely-viewed YouTube videos featuring the song clip. The boombox itself – and the video, which features the boombox sitting in a pink, fluffy environment – have nothing to do with the song or with the adult film in which it was featured. It was chosen just because the poster felt like it fit the "vibe" of the song.

"It's kind of like – wow! The universe shifted, and it's like, 'You guys have got to do some '80s music, boom," Booth added.

"This had been going on since 2021, and we had no idea," Philip Adrian Booth added. "On April 28th, they put names to the lost song, and then our phones and social media and the news and everyone started texting us, like, 'Did you know this is going on?' My daughter said, 'This is all over TikTok.' To hear it from your kids is pretty amazing. It's like, 'You're all over, we're so proud of you.'"
Christopher chimed in to add, "My son Gabriel, he's 16 so he's a big social media, Redditor, TikToker, and he went, 'Dad, you're God on the internet,' and I went 'What?' And then he showed me and he said he was really proud. You always want to impress your family, your children, and it made me very proud. But it's still very – it's numbing. It's a foggy thing. I don't think it's really sunk in still."

The song is catchy – so much so that it quickly became one of the most sought-after lost songs on the internet, and the search got its own subreddit – ironically called "Everyone Knows That." The irony? Per the Booth brothers and the original lyrics they unearthed, the lyrics actually say "everyone knows *it*," not "that." The most common way to refer to the song was the result of a misheard lyric.

"When it first happened and we started looking at the Reddit, and there were so many of those people – so many internet sleuths – and going on TikTok and seeing all of those people singing our song and miming our song...I can't describe how rewarding that is," Philip told us.

"It's like our version of going into an arena, and 40,000 people were singing your song," Christopher added."

"It's a positive, incredible experience," Philip added. "In today's world, things like that just don't happen, so our heads are still spinning from it all. We first thought, 'What's the next step?'"

The pair have projects – musically and in the film and TV space – that are already in progress, but almost immediately after they learned of "Ulterior Motives" having viral success, they dedicated themselves to getting the song released. In fact, while digging through old files and master tapes, they have decided to put together an album of their unreleased 1980s pop material, hoping that fans will be excited by more than just the mystery behind one song.

"I sat in the studio, and I'm still going through old

CDs and cassettes – the quality of a cassette now that's kept for 40 years is diminished – but I'm still going through stuff and finding tracks that we did then. I'm still searching for the vocals for 'Ulterior Motives,'" Christopher said. "We do have the rhythm track, and it sounds great, but we don't have the lead guitar, the synth hits, and we don't have the vocals. But since I'm the singer, I can copy most of it. So we're going to look for it, and if not, we're going to go in and re-record the parts. Part of it is going to be 100% original."

Christopher added that the MIDI guitar used on the original track is also one he still owns, so if they can't find the originals, he has the best gear possible to replicate the sound as closely as he can. While the pair have obviously grown as artists in the intervening decades, they don't want to put too much of a spin on the first commercial release for "Ulterior Motives." Instead, they would rather give the audience exactly what they're expecting – or as exactly as they possibly can.

"I think it's important to keep the same flavor," Philip said. "I think how to adapt that is, give the people what they want and keep it as original as you can, and then maybe do an EP version and slam a couple of remixes on it. That way they can get what they want, and what they don't want, they don't have to listen to."

Like nearly everyone who works in "genre" film and TV, Christopher and Philip Booth spend a fair amount of time at fan conventions. It's an interesting time, because in addition to the normal fans of their more recent work onscreen, Christopher has been posting photos from signing appearances where they have been posing with pink boomboxes.

"There's millions of views on TikTok videos, and I know that all of my social media sites have quadrupled with many new, younger fans,"

Christopher told us. "Music is our first love, and never quit music. Even when we do movies, I do all of the soundtracks, and I've invested a lot in my studio. Obviously, we have commitments, and we're going to finish those, but at the same time, there's absolutely no way we can walk away from this."

"This kind of thing doesn't just happen," Philip added. "It seems like a big injustice not to take advantage of the situation, all these people, it makes them so happy, and the high of seeing them sing it or whatever, there's no better feeling than that....We put many decades into music, and we've been doing it a long time. Chris and I go way back to a band, here's some trivia for you, a band called Sweeney Todd. And they were really big in Canada, and they had a hit song in the late '70s, early '80s, called Roxy Roller. And the lead singer was a guy named Nick Gilder, and he had 'Hot Child in the City,' and he sold and wrote songs to Scandal, they were very '80s. And then, Bryan Adams replaced him. And then, when Bryan Adams left the band, Chris replaced him as a singer, and I replaced as a guitar player. And we played with our brother who was the original member of Sweeney Todd. And that's kind of how all this got started in the early '80s We had some pretty big success back then in bands."

"I remember the day I turned 18, I was playing for

20,000 people in an arena," Christopher added.

The two recalled that, in the early days of their time living in the U.S., they opened for Motley Crue and played big venues like The Troubadour and The Roxy, getting to know the likes of Vince Neil and U2.

"We have done a lot of things after that and musically, and even singing-wise, I got a lot better," Christopher told us, adding that since the tapes used for "Ulterior Motives" may have even been demos, the song itself is a little rough around the edges. "It's not perfect. There was no Auto-Tune, at all, so it is what it is. But, at the same time, I'm listening to all these people singing this song and loving it, and I'm finding I'm singing it, and it's our own song. Maybe back then we didn't even care for it, because you know how you are. But now we love it, so I'm really pumped to do a whole '80s album at this point."

After years of searching, digging through copyright filings, bugging members of other bands, and all the general dead ends of a lost media search, some fans were exasperated to discover "Ulterior Motives" on an adult film (1986's *Angels of Passion*). The Booths say they didn't write the song for the movie, but that some of their music ended up in adult films simply because it was a way to make some extra money off unused material.

"We've never really written for adult films," Christopher said. "We were musicians, and we needed money. A friend of ours was, at that time, was making what were very big budget adult films — they were $250,000.00 a film. These guys were making them, and we didn't know anything about it, but it was like, 'Hey, do you want to make a couple extra hundred dollars today and help move equipment or do this?' and I went, 'Sure. It don't matter to me. We just need to pay the rent.' We just went and did our job and walked out, when they started doing their nastiness, we never really hung around. And then, they said, 'Hey, we need some music. Do you got any music?' so I said, 'Yeah, we've got some music,' because what we did is we took all that money and bought better equipment, old Fostex boards, and it kept going and going and going."

Philip said that it was a great experience for them – one that would pay off later in their film career – to see productions of that scope at work. Comparing the productions to *Boogie Nights*, Philip said that the movies were all shot on film at that point, and then mixed with "like 128 tracks" on huge sound stages.

"Actually, there was two tracks of music and 126 tracks of moaning and groaning, but they would mix these on these huge screens and sound stages," Christopher joked.

More seriously, he added, "We were never really bored. I would just go into studio and I would sit down and write music. And, of course, I was always a romantic, and my music was always kind of sexy, so they liked it. I don't know how you can write music to a hardcore sex scene, you know? Unless you're Nine Inch Nails, 'Closer,' which is very cool as well. A lot of people made fun of us, and they still do, and I get that. But, at the same time, when I became a businessman, I went ahead and registered all those songs with the BMI, and they turned all those films into erotic thrillers, and I got an incredible amount of royalties for the music over the next 10 years. So, I felt really good about being a musician, making money."

And the next step is getting back to that a little bit. The "businessman" side has had to step forward a bit since the song was found, especially since the pair are worried that all the copycats and unauthorized covers – and now, dubs from the movie – that are circulating online might make it harder for them to monetize any music videos and digital sales once the new album hits. They're reaching out to fans to ask that they pause on uploading that kind of thing while the record is finished and the original song can finally be released for the first time. In the meantime, it sounds like they won't have to go totally on their own for the project.

"We have been asked by record companies to do it on vinyl and back on cassette, because I know cassette is making a comeback," Christopher said. "I think that we'll do is, we'll go ahead and get all the tracks ready and we'll get 'Ulterior Motives' in a good place. And then, we'll have some of the other tracks, in case people want to hear more. Obviously, streaming is a tough business to make any monetary gain out of it, but it's instant gratification for people streaming. I love CDs still, and I love vinyl. I print everything I do on CDs. I haven't done a vinyl yet, but I definitely think that this music could be savvy for that."

Philip added, "I think if they love the hook of 'Ulterior Motives,' we've got quite a few songs that we were listening to, that are just as amazing. It opens up that door, because I can only imagine, if you love that song, how much you're going to love this other one. It's definitely busy, while we're making our films and doing that, I don't think we can walk away from this. I think we have to seriously look and say, 'We've got to make time for this,' because this doesn't happen every day. You don't get notoriety like that every day. I think it's important to give those people — they made us feel like a million dollars when this happened — and I think we need to return the favor and release this song, exactly how they liked it.

And if they want more, we've got more."

EVERYONE KNOWS IT! Our 8os song ended up in an X-rated movie – we were clueless it became an internet mystery & now it's revived our career.

By Cheyenne R. Ubiera, Night News Reporter

While this mystery was solved there are still searches for other songs that continue.

A SIMPLE request to find the name of a forgotten song from the 1980s launched a three-year search that ended with an unlikely result and saw twin musicians thrust into social media stardom.

Christopher Saint Booth and Philip Adrian Booth are lifelong musicians and filmmakers who have worked on projects throughout their decades-long careers.Christopher Saint Booth and Philip Adrian Booth had no idea a song they made 40 years ago would become part of an internet search.

In the 1980s, the identical twin brothers were in their early 20s and worked odd jobs in the entertainment industry, which often included licensing some of their songs to adult film producers.

"It wasn't written for the movie. It was just someone saying, 'Hey dude, I need some music you have to use. Whatever it is,'" Christopher told The U.S. Sun. Many of the adult films the brothers did music for were turned into "erotic thrillers," which were shown on networks such as Cinemax and Showtime.

The money they made from the royalties helped

launch their careers, which have largely turned into horror films and paranormal documentaries. The brothers, admittedly, were confused about what the fuss was about as they only used social media to promote their upcoming projects.

"My daughter texted me and said, 'I'm so proud of you guys,'" said Philip.

The brothers have been musicians and filmmakers since the 1980s, performing under the name Who's Who?

"I've been in the entertainment business for so long but we still didn't really understand the concept of social media."

The brothers' accounts were flooded with comments and followers with Christopher gaining roughly 36,000 followers in about 30 days.
It all stemmed from a song they recorded in 1983, Ulterior Motives, which was licensed for the 1986 pornographic film Angels of Passion.

Nearly 40 years since the film's release, the Booths had completely forgotten about the song and had no idea it had been part of a popular internet search.
"I think it's super cool, but I wasn't knowledgeable at all," said Christopher.
"I think it's amazing that people do that, you know. The only thing we knew was that they found this song...I didn't even recognize the title until I heard the song."

A NEW SEARCH

The search for Ulterior Motives started on October

7, 2021, when a user only identified as Carl92 posted on the song identification website WatZatSong, asking others to identify a snippet that he found. The 17-second snippet was muffled, making it hard to recognize the lyrics, prompting users to call the song Everyone Knows That or EKT.

During the three-year search, Reddit users joined in and created a subreddit dedicated to posting potential leads in hopes of solving the lost media riddle.

Before the song's eventual discovery, several theories were posted in the subreddit as some people doubted the song's authenticity.
Some believed the entire thing was a hoax created by Carl92, accusing him of generating the song using artificial intelligence.

In October 2021, Carl92 posted on WatZatSong, claiming that he found a recording in an old DVD backup.

Carl92 shared a 17-second snippet of the song in the forum and answered a few questions on how he discovered it, writing, "Probably I was simply learning how to capture audio and this was a leftover."

The song became one of the most infamous mysteries on WatZatSong with the original post receiving the most comments since the site launched in 2006.

Carl92 eventually stopped posting after users asked him several invasion questions but the search soon gained popularity on Reddit adding thousands more into the mix. A new subreddit was created exclusively dedicated to the search for the song in June 2023.

In August 2023, user HeyScarlett found a song registered under the name Ulterior Movies in the Society of Composers, Authors and Music Publishers of Canada (SOCAN) database.

Using HeyScarlett's lead, Reddit user South_Pole_ball identified the song on April 28, 2024, along with the names of the Booth brothers as the songwriters.

Others suggested that Carl92 was affiliated with WatZatSong and made the post to increase web traffic to the site with the search.

Finally, on April 28, 2024, Reddit user South_Pole_Ball shared a video on r/EveryoneKnowsThat of the full song.

The discovery sparked a new search as users have asked the brothers to release a studio version of Ulterior Motives but the Booths say that's easier said than done.

"We're very well prepared to go in the studio and re-record it vocally," said Christopher.

"We have quite an impressive studio in our house and started pulling up tracks without digging too deep," Philip added.

"We started listening for where she could find this track and came across a lot of our eighties stuff that we recorded at the time."

The brothers said they would likely re-record the vocals if they couldn't find the vocal tracks but shared that they still have the same equipment from the 1980s.

"Everybody said, 'How do you get that guitar sound?' and at the time it was a MIDI guitar, where you're triggering keyboards at the same time you're running the outpost of a regular guitar," said Philip.

If it's a true search, then we need to deliver. We are embracing what happened and are so humbled by this.....Philip Adrian Booth

"So it's gonna be a lot of fun. It's been such an uncertain, surreal experience."
Philip also clarified that the lyrics that Redditors used to identify the song were incorrect.

"The real words are 'Everyone knows it,' not 'that.'"

While the brothers are the most recent case of "lost-wave," a term used to describe music with little to no information about its origins, they aren't the only ones.

In 2016, the British indie rock band, Panchiko, gained attention after their 2000 demo extended play, or EP, D>E>A>T>H>M>E>T>A>L, was discovered at a thrift store and gained a cult following.

Online users were able to track down the band members, who had broken up in 2001 and had no idea that people were looking for them.
The band reformed in 2020 and now has over one

million monthly listeners on Spotify.

However, another song known as The Most Mysterious Song on the Internet, which many believe was recorded in the early 1980s, remains unsolved.

While the brothers have enjoyed all the new attention they've received, not all of it has been great.

Several fake videos have been posted to YouTube and other platforms claiming to be the official version of Ulterior Motives.
"I think it's important to address that anybody telling you or promoting that the song is out is lying," said Christopher.

"It has not been released by us. A lot of people have put it up [on YouTube] and a few have even remade it with the wrong lyrics and different musicians." Philip called it "a little frustrating and disappointing" that some have tried to take credit for the song, saying that it was disrespectful to the online community who searched so long to find the track.

What is lost media?

Lost media is any media (books, films, TV shows, songs, video games, etc.) that either no longer exists in any format or is not available to the public.

In the early days of filmmaking, many shows and radio broadcasts were recorded on magnetic tapes that were either lost or destroyed. It was also an industry standard to tape over, or "junk," previous recordings.

Formats such as film, tape, CDs, DVDs, and digital data stored on hard drives also naturally decay over time if they're not kept in proper storage conditions. In modern times, websites, livestreams, and blog posts that aren't properly archived can also be lost if the website is shut down or deleted by the creator. Lost media restoration is often fronted through online communities or dedicated databases Source: ...Lost Media Wiki.

"If it's a true search, then we need to deliver," he said. "We are embracing what happened and are so humbled by this.

"The least we can do for all the support, and we've had millions and millions of people reach out to us, is put out a version that's not half-a**ed."
There have also been new theories that have come out since the brothers came forward as the musicians behind Ulterior Motives from the brothers being AI-generated to Christopher being a 13-year-old Japanese girl.

"Back then the vocals were high but I am the real singer and for me to re-record it is going to be a bit of a challenge because you grow older, your style changes, your body changes, and your voice changes," he said.

"But I'm pretty sure I'm going to be able to do most of it. Maybe with the high notes I'm going to have to, you know, really squeal to do it."

The Booths are hoping to have the song ready for a summer release but are still wary of any obstacles they'll have to go through. However, since they found other tracks from the 1980s, they've been playing around with the idea of releasing an EP, with three or four more tracks. "It would be wonderful if everybody wanted that," said Christopher.

THE BOOTH BROTHERS (Village Recorder-Los Angeles)

TOYS (1976)

AFFAIR (1982)

THE BOOTH BROTHERS (2024)

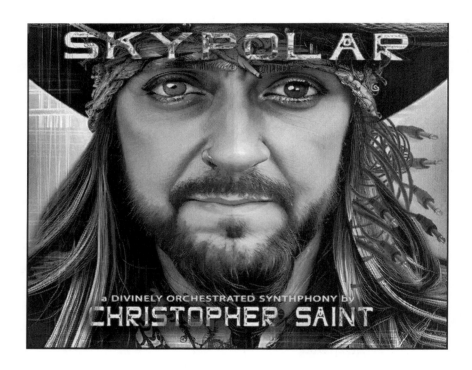

SKYPOLAR NOW STREAMING

Booth Brothers Winner of over 11 awards

The Movies

Music has always been our first love, but the creative passion of creating from a visual storytelling side fascinated us. This took us deep into the chapter of our lives in world of writing, scoring, editing, producing, directing and filming our own feature films and documentaries. Fun fact, You will even see us on screen in several of them.

In 2000 we decided to use our own funding to create our very first feature film. As children we loved the Hammer films that we used to watch as kids so we embarked out on creating a horror film called DARKPLACE. This would star Matthew McGrory well known as Tiny from the Rob Zombie movies, "House of a 1000 corpses and Devil's Rejects". Also Katherine Boecher from the hit series "Supernatural "and Timothy Lee Depriest from hit show "WestWorld. This was

well received and spawned a SAG (Screen Actors Guild Award) for best independent screenplay and went on to win numerous film festivals.

The success of that film led us further in the horror film world to create "Death Tunnel" for Sony Pictures, filmed at one of the most haunted Asylums in America. This became a cult classic and is available in over 70 countries worldwide. After a NBC/Universal executive spotted us at a film convention, he approached us with proposal , make us a show of what it was like for horror filmmakers to have real supernatural events happen while making a horror film. This became "Spooked, The Ghosts of Waverly Hills Sanatorium, for the SyFy channel and the Booth Brothers TV persona was born.

From then on we did multiple films and documentaries for TV and streaming platforms including " The Possessed, Children of the Grave, The Exorcist File- Haunted Boy", the real life story that inspired the motion picture " The Exorcist. Also "Dead Still, Soul Catcher, Trail of Fears,"The Attached and our brand new film, "Never Blink "

The music was also an essential part of these motion pictures in turn driving the cinematic visuals, now recognized worldwide as the unique Booth Brothers style. They all been very successful and we are eternally grateful to all who watched and supported us along the way. You can see these films on Apple+, Tubi, Prime Video,The Roku Channel and more.

...Philip Booth

SPECIAL THANKS TO OUR FANS

Lyrics translation by Nicole Rose Sacks
Pictures Tom Pendell, Christopher & Philip Booth and Tom Feske

ROCKERS' REVENGE: follically mutant Yorkshire twins Chris and Phil O'Toole, who run one of the world's biggest companies

Made in the USA
Columbia, SC
18 November 2024

46433181R00065